READING STUDIES FOR DRUMS AND PERCUSSION

Ron Delp

Berklee Press

Vice President: David Kusek
Dean of Continuing Education: Debbie Cavalier
Chief Operating Officer: Robert F. Green
Managing Editor: Jonathan Feist
Editorial Assistants: Yousun Choi, Emily Goldstein, Claudia Obser
Cover Designer: Kathy Kikkert
Cover Photo: Phil Farnsworth

ISBN 978-1-4234-6688-8

DISTRIBUTED BY

HAL•LEONARD®
CORPORATION
7777 W. BLUEMOUND RD. P.O. BOX 13819
MILWAUKEE, WISCONSIN 53213

1140 Boylston Street
Boston, MA 02215-3693 USA
(617) 747-2146

Visit Berklee Press Online at
www.berkleepress.com

Visit Hal Leonard Online at
www.halleonard.com

DIRECTIONS FOR PLAYING

As mentioned before, the following studies should commence only when the student can adequately handle the new material in each study when notated on a single line.

The new material contained in each study is listed in the upper right-hand corner of the page.

NO METRONOME MARKINGS are given so that the student can begin and progress at his own rate. A steady tempo is, of course, a must!

STICKING is not included in the studies. At the outset, the student might be better off playing any way he can. Many possible stickings exist, but the student will learn to make the best choice on his own. The study of rudiments and a good stick control text (such as George Stone's *Stick Control*) will certainly help.

THERE IS NO INDICATION AS TO INSTRUMENTATION. The unique factor in being a percussionist is that one can, and will often have to, play on a wide variety of instrument combinations. Therefore, in this book the student can play the two, three, four, or five pitches wherever he likes.

Tuned drums would be the logical choice, but it is suggested that the player use wood blocks, cymbals, cowbells, etc. and different combinations of instruments for variety of sound, playing surface (rebound), and physical space between instruments. Some possibilities might be:

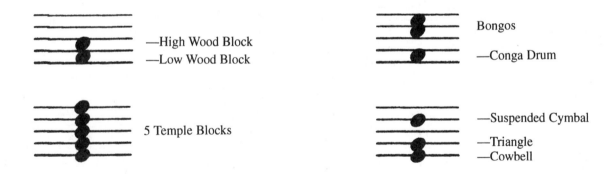

FOR THE STUDENT WHO DOES NOT POSSESS THE NECESSARY INSTRUMENTS, books, pots and pans, practice pads, and even his music stand could be used to substitute for conventional instruments.

In performance, most players set up their instruments in order from left to right according to WRITTEN pitch. In other words, the lowest pitch corresponds to the instruments on the far left, the highest pitch is on the far right.

THE DRUM SET

These studies can be performed in many ways on the drum set. Here are some ideas:

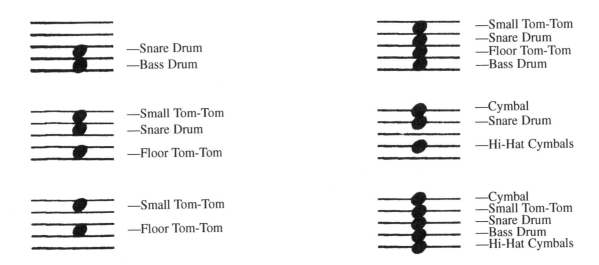

A cymbal part can be added, played with the right hand, while the written notes are played with the left and the feet:

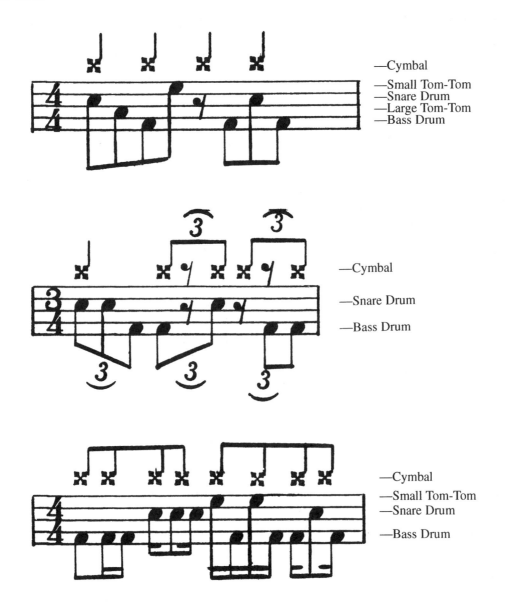

Two Pitches

1

New Material:

Two Pitches

2

New Material: None

3

Three Pitches

New Material: None

4

Three Pitches

5

Two Pitches

New Material:

Three Pitches

6

New Material: None

7

Two Pitches

New Material: ⸰

8

Three Pitches

New Material: None

9

Two Pitches

New Material:

Tie Syncopation

10

Three Pitches

New Material: None

11

Two Pitches

New Material: The Dot

12

Three Pitches

New Material: None

13

Three Pitches

New Material: None

14

Two Pitches

New Material:

15

Two Pitches

New Material: None

16

Three Pitches

New Material: None

17

Two Pitches

New Material:

18

Three Pitches

New Material: None

19

Two Pitches

New Material:

20

Three Pitches

New Material: None

21

Three Pitches

New Material: None

22

Two Pitches

New Material:

23

Two Pitches

New Material: None

24

Three Pitches

New Material: None

25

Three Pitches

New Material: ⁊ ♪.

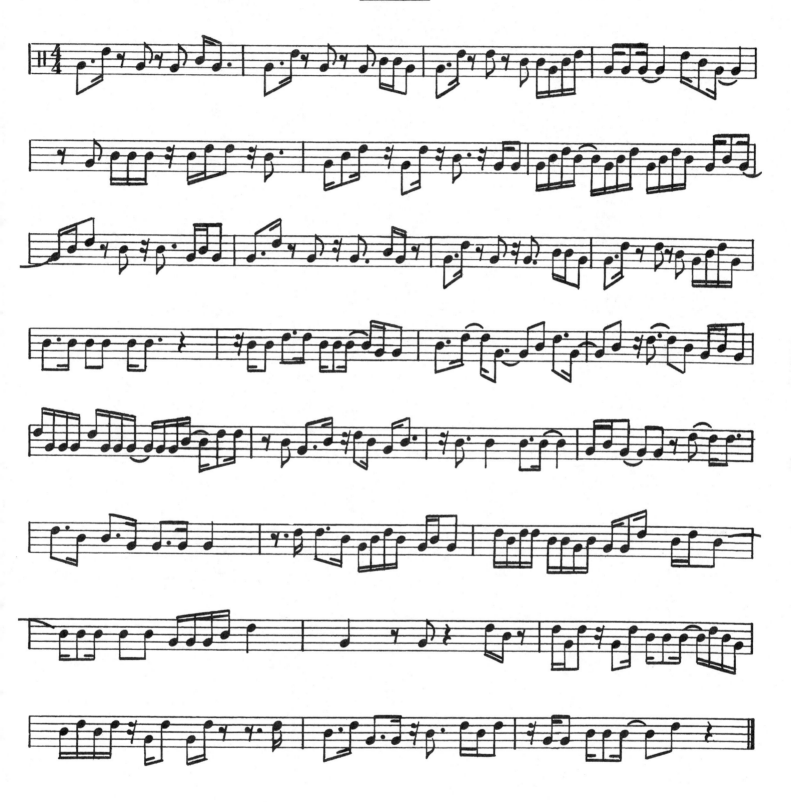

26

Two Pitches

New Material:

27

Two Pitches

New Material: None

28

Two Pitches

30

Three Pitches

New Material: None

31

Three Pitches

32

Four Pitches  Combination Study

33

Four Pitches

Combination Study

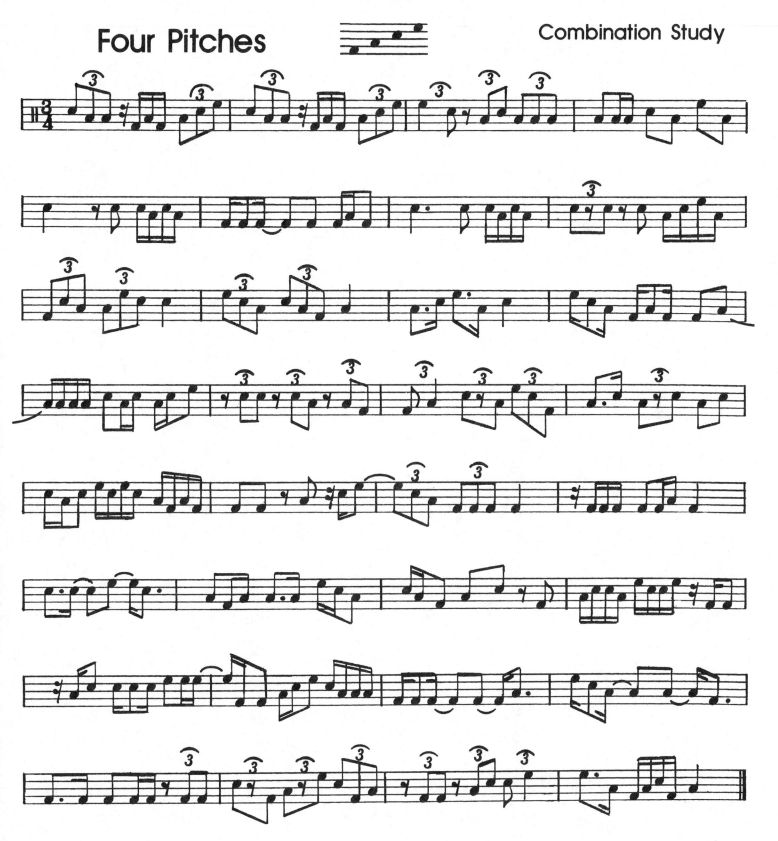

34

Four Pitches

Combination Study

35

Five Pitches

Combination Study

36

Five Pitches  Combination Study

37

Five Pitches

Combination Study

38

Five Pitches

Combination Study

39

Four Pitches

Double Stops ♩ = R.H. ♪ = L.H.

40

Five Pitches

Double Stops

41

Four Pitches

Double Stops

42

Three Pitches

Changing Meter

$\quad \downarrow = \downarrow$ Throughout

43

Four Pitches

44

Five Pitches

Changing Meter